Andrew Johnson

Andrew Johnson

Don Nardo

AMERICA'S
17TH
PRESIDENT

Children's Press®
A Division of Scholastic Inc.
New York / Toronto / London / Auckland / Sydney
Mexico City / New Delhi / Hong Kong
Danbury, Connecticut

Library of Congress Cataloging-in-Publication Data

Nardo, Don, 1947–
    Andrew Johnson / by Don Nardo.
      p. cm. — (Encyclopedia of presidents. Second series)
    Summary: A biography of the man who became the seventeenth president
of the United States following the assassination of Abraham Lincoln, providing
information on his childhood, education, family, political career, time as president, and legacy.
Includes bibliographical references and index.
  ISBN 0-516-24242-3
   1. Johnson, Andrew, 1808–1875—Juvenile literature. 2. Presidents—United
States—Biography—Juvenile literature. [1. Johnson, Andrew, 1808–1875.
2. Presidents.] I. Title. II. Series.
E667.N37 2004
973.8'1'092—dc22

                                        2003015920

Contents

Chapter 1

An Unlikely Story

Andrew Johnson followed a surprising path to the presidency of the United States. He suffered many hardships in his youth and was largely self-educated, yet he found early success as a local political leader. Later, he served as member of the U.S. House of Representatives and governor of his state. By 1860, he was a U.S. senator.

In spite of this success, it seemed certain that Johnson would not rise to a higher office. The country, torn by the issues of slavery and states' rights, elected Republican Abraham Lincoln to be president. Lincoln and his party opposed the spread of slavery and seemed hostile to the South. Johnson was a Democrat and represented Tennessee in the Senate. He usually voted with other southern Democrats to preserve slavery and protect the rights of individual states.

Then, in a series of surprising turnabouts, Johnson became a hero to most northerners and a villain to most southerners. When southern states began seceding from the Union, Johnson denounced them. When his own state seceded, he remained in the Senate, loyal to the Union. In 1864 Lincoln's Republican party nominated Democrat Andrew Johnson to run for vice president on the ticket with Lincoln. They won, and Johnson became vice president.

The turnabouts continued. Weeks after Johnson was sworn in as vice president, Abraham Lincoln was shot and killed by an assassin. Andrew Johnson was sworn in as president. He took office as a southerner in a country ruled by the northern states. His own region was defeated and war-torn, and its states had no representatives in the federal government. He was a Democrat sharing power with a Republican Congress at a moment when the government faced some of the most difficult problems in its history. How could the states of the North and South be put back together after decades of division and four years of furious battle? What must the southern states do to regain their place in the Union? What should be done about four million former slaves, now free? Finally, who should decide these huge questions, the president or Congress?

At this point, fortune turned against Andrew Johnson. He believed he had good answers for the country's problems, but he soon found himself in a personal war against the competing answers of the Republican Congress. Johnson proposed a plan for reconstructing the Union, and Congress overturned it. Congress passed its own plan, and Johnson vetoed it. Congress passed its own plan again, overriding his veto. It passed a law limiting the president's right to appoint or fire high officials in the government. Johnson defied the law, and Congress put him on trial, seeking to remove him from office.

Johnson escaped removal from office, but in nearly every way he was the loser. Congress and most of the country had turned against him, and he had been forced to give up nearly all the powers of the presidency. How could a single political leader rise so high and fall so far in a few short years? The story of Andrew Johnson is one of the most dramatic, and perhaps the most tragic, of all the presidents.

Beginnings

Andrew Johnson was born on December 29, 1808, in Raleigh, North Carolina. He was the second son of Jacob Johnson, a poor laborer, and his wife Mary (nicknamed Polly). In January 1812, when Andrew was three and his brother William was eight, their father jumped into an icy river to help rescue three men who had fallen in. The three men were saved, but Jacob fell ill and died shortly afterward. He left his grieving wife and two young sons.

Andrew Johnson was born in this small building behind a tavern in Raleigh, North Carolina. The building has been moved to a historical park in Raleigh.

Jacob's heroism did not help his family. His death left Polly Johnson to support herself and her children, then a very difficult task for a single woman. She made a few pennies by doing other people's laundry and by spinning thread.

Jacob Johnson's Heroism

One of the men Jacob rescued from drowning was Thomas Henderson, publisher of the *Raleigh Star*. Grateful to his rescuer, Henderson printed the following notice in his January 12, 1812, edition:

Died, in this city on Saturday last, Jacob Johnson, who for many years occupied a humble but useful station. He was the city constable, sexton and porter [doorman] to the State Bank. . . . He was esteemed for his honesty, sobriety, industry, and his humane, friendly disposition. Among all [to] whom he was known and esteemed, none lament him, except perhaps his own relatives, more than the publisher of this newspaper, for he owes his life on a particular occasion to the kindness and humanity of Johnson.

☆ ☆ ☆

Later that year, she married Turner Haughtry. The family remained poor, and was scarcely able to make ends meet.

Apprenticeship

The Johnson boys' mother and stepfather decided to apprentice them to a local tailor, a tradesman who made and altered clothes. A young apprentice became a lowly assistant to a tradesman, receiving food and shelter in return for hours of hard work each day. At the age of ten, two years after his father died, William went to work for Raleigh tailor James Selby. When Andrew turned ten, he was apprenticed to Selby as well.

Apprenticeship was a good way for a boy to learn a trade. After years of training, he could open his own shop, make a good living, and perhaps take on apprentices of his own. Yet apprentices often worked under harsh and difficult conditions. They were required to obey their master and could be punished severely for misbehavior or poor work. They had few ways to complain of mistreatment. Worst of all, most apprenticeship agreements required an apprentice to work for his master until he turned 21 years old.

At first, Andrew may have found his apprenticeship challenging. He did learn his trade and would later support his family for years as a tailor. After five years, however, he felt trapped in his situation. He complained especially that there was no time for school. He was trying hard to learn to read and write, but there was so much work to do that he made slow progress.

In June 1824, when Andrew was nearly 16, he and his brother played a boyhood prank that went awry. When the victim of the prank threatened to sue, the Johnson brothers decided to run away from Raleigh and from Selby's tailor shop. They traveled first to Carthage, a small town about 50 miles (80 kilometers) southwest of Raleigh. James Selby paid for advertisements in local papers, hoping that someone would recognize his runaway apprentices and return them.

James Selby published this advertisement on June 24, 1824:

TEN DOLLARS REWARD. Ran away . . . on the night of the 15th . . . two apprentice boys, legally bound, WILLIAM AND ANDREW JOHNSON. The former is of dark complexion, black hair, eyes. . . . The latter is very fleshy, freckled face, light hair, and fair complexion. . . . When they went away they were clad [in] blue cloth coats . . . and new hats. I will pay the above reward to any person who will deliver said apprentices to me in Raleigh, or I will give the above reward for Andrew Johnson alone. All persons are cautioned against harboring or employing said apprentices, on pain of being prosecuted.

As the advertisement suggests, it would be illegal for the Johnson boys to work for anyone else, since they were legally apprenticed to Selby. Oddly, Selby mixed up the boys' descriptions, as Andrew was the dark-complexioned one.

☆ ★ ☆

After only a few months, Andrew left Carthage and moved to Laurens, South Carolina. He was safer there, since North Carolina apprenticeship laws could not be enforced in another state. He found a position in a small tailor's shop, but he missed his family and felt uncomfortable as a fugitive. So early in 1826, he decided it was time to return to Raleigh and clear his name. When he approached his former master about paying off the rest of his apprenticeship contract, Selby demanded a large sum of money.

A New Beginning

Johnson did not have that kind of money. Yet he was still legally bound to Selby, who would be able to seize any money he earned. Johnson thought the best plan would be to head west across the mountains and seek his fortune in Tennessee. His mother and stepfather decided to go with him. In August 1826, they left Raleigh with a single horse-drawn cart of belongings.

A month later, the family arrived in Greeneville, a town in the mountains of eastern Tennessee, and decided to stay. For a few months Johnson worked for a local tailor. Then in March 1827, 18-year-old Andrew opened his own business. He proudly hung a sign over the door reading "A. Johnson Tailor Shop."

Johnson soon made a name for himself in Greeneville. He became friends with many local tradesmen and farmers. In the east Tennessee hill country, there were no large plantations and rich plantation owners. Tradesmen and farmers had a strong voice in local politics, and they enjoyed debating the major issues of the day. Andrew was not a fast reader or a good writer, but he soon learned to be a persuasive speaker and debater.

Andrew Johnson operated his tailor's shop in this small frame building in Greeneville, Tennessee.

Not long after arriving in Greeneville, Johnson met Eliza McCardle, the daughter of a shoemaker. Only months after he opened his tailor shop, Andrew and Eliza were married on May 17, 1827. He was 18 and she was 16. Eliza was a bright young woman who was a much better reader and writer than Andrew. After their marriage, she helped him learn how to read and spell month after month, often teaching him as he stitched clothes in his shop.

Champion of the Common Man

Andrew Johnson's interest in local politics continued to grow. His shop became a gathering place for discussion. He began paying a young man 50 cents a day to read newspaper articles and political speeches to him as he worked. In the spring of 1829, Johnson decided to run for alderman, one of the members of the board of aldermen, or town council. He won, and was reelected to the board each of the next seven years. Twice, the other aldermen elected him mayor, or chairman of the board meetings, for the year.

Johnson began to make a name for himself in neighboring towns. In 1835, he ran for the seat representing the Greeneville region in the state legislature. He ran proudly as a Democrat, a member of the recently reorganized party led by Tennesseean Andrew Jackson, who was president of the United States. Together with other Democrats, Johnson was suspicious of merchants, businessmen, and banks. He believed that government should be as small as possible. With Jackson, he was a strong believer in the worth and rights of ordinary small farmers and tradesmen like the ones in his home district. In the legislature he fought against high taxes and regulations that hurt common people.

The Old College building at Tusculum College in Greeneville. Johnson never studied at the school, but he did participate in political debates there and later contributed to the school's building fund. Today this building is the Andrew Johnson Museum and Library.

In other parts of Tennessee, where there were large plantations and wealthy landowners, the Whig party was strong. It supported a larger, more active government that would help improve transportation and increase business and trade. Johnson was an outspoken critic of Whig ideas and of the men who supported them.

In 1840, Johnson rose another step on the political ladder, gaining election to the Tennessee state senate. In his two-year term, he stuck to his principles. One bill proposed the construction of a new paved road that would pass through his own district, helping the people he represented. Since the plan was to construct the road at taxpayer expense, however, Johnson opposed it. He believed that those who used the road should pay for it, not the poor who could not afford to pay higher taxes. He also opposed large government grants to railroad companies, which were beginning to build tracks throughout the state.

Bound for Washington

In 1842, Johnson broke out of Tennessee politics and was elected to represent his east Tennessee district in the U.S. House of Representatives in Washington, D.C. He arrived in Congress at a time when the Democratic party was out of power, and the Whigs had a majority in the House. He was no more impressed with the Whigs in Washington than with those in Nashville.

Johnson was especially upset by the eagerness of the Whigs to increase government spending. Time and again he voted against bills to establish new programs, even when they seemed helpful. He continued to believe that the best government is a small government. Other congressmen saw him as deeply conservative and against progress. His beliefs and his voting record pleased his district, however. They elected him to five two-year terms.

The Capitol in Washington, D.C., at about the time Johnson arrived to serve in the House of Representatives.

In his House career, Johnson voted against creating the now famous national museum, the Smithsonian Institution; against expanding the U.S. patent office, which registered new inventions; and against federal spending for improved roads and railroads. He tried to reduce the number of federal employees and even supported cutting the salaries of congressmen, including himself. On one occasion, he returned $216 to the federal treasury, saying he had been over-paid for travel expenses.

Andrew Johnson

Johnson's one positive proposal as a congressman was a homestead bill. He first proposed it in 1846. It called for giving small plots of undeveloped government land to new settlers in the West. Settlers would be given temporary title to the land. If they cleared and farmed it for five years, they would receive full ownership. The bill was opposed by business interests in the northern states and by plantation owners in the South, and went down to defeat. Johnson continued to introduce it, however, never seeming to get discouraged. In July 1850, he told the House, "[The homestead bill] will make many a poor man's heart rejoice. Pass this bill and their wives and children will invoke blessings on your heads. Pass this bill, and millions now unborn will look back with wonder and admiration upon the age in which it was done."

Governor of Tennessee

In 1852, Johnson's Whig opponents in Tennessee redrew his congressional district in a way that made it impossible for him to gain reelection. Combative as ever, he arranged to gain the Democratic nomination for governor. In the election, he defeated the Whig leader who had redrawn his congressional district. Two years later, after a bruising campaign, Johnson was reelected to a second two-year term as governor.

Johnson used his position as governor to promote his positive proposals for the state. He called for a major expansion of public education, hoping to make free public schools available to the thousands of children whose families could not afford to pay for private schools. He also spoke out for a state version of a homestead bill, giving small parcels of land to settlers who would clear and farm them. Unfortunately, a Tennessee governor had few powers, and Johnson failed to get his proposals enacted by the legislature.

By 1857, Johnson was eager to return to Washington. During his last year as governor, he campaigned for election to the U.S. Senate from Tennessee. In those days, U.S. senators were elected by state legislatures. Johnson won the Democratic nomination and was elected. Once more he would be involved in national affairs.

Chapter 2

Proud New Senator

As Tennessee's new senator in 1857, Andrew Johnson seemed to be at the peak of a successful career. In the public arena, he had successfully served both his state and his country in numerous capacities. He also had a happy marriage and a big family. He and Eliza had five children. Four of them were now young adults: Martha (born in 1828), Charles (1830), Mary (1832), and Robert (1834). Andrew Jr., nicknamed Frank, had been born in 1852 and was the much admired "baby" of the family.

Johnson's immediate goal as a senator was to promote his homestead bill, which after many years of debate had still not passed both houses of Congress. To him, the need for this program of land distribution seemed clear. Johnson believed that small farmers were the key to the country's prosperity and future. The promising lands west of the Mississippi River were still being settled, and the federal government owned the lands not yet claimed. The country would be strengthened by encouraging settlers to clear new lands and make them productive. As in his earlier bills, Johnson proposed that settlers be given temporary title to a homestead and be granted full ownership if they cleared the land and farmed it for five years. He believed that farms could become a new source of prosperity for future generations of Americans.

Johnson's proposal was opposed by the new railroad companies. They were receiving huge grants of government land themselves. They used a small part of the land for the railroad tracks, then hoped to sell the remaining land to settlers. If settlers could get free land from the government, the railroads' lands would be worth much less.

Even more strongly opposed were the political leaders of the southern states. They saw the act as a way to break up huge tracts of land into small farms rather than large plantations that might be cultivated profitably with slaves. During Johnson's campaign for the Homestead Act, disputes about whether slavery would be allowed in western territories were creating growing conflict between North and South. Southern congressmen saw Johnson's plan as one that would favor the North, and they considered him an enemy rather than a friend.

Even against this powerful opposition, Johnson and his allies succeeded in passing the Homestead Act in both houses of Congress in July 1860. Johnson was deeply disappointed when Democratic president James Buchanan *vetoed* the act two days later, refusing to sign it into law. (Two years later, after Johnson had left the Senate, Congress passed the Homestead Act, and it was signed into law by President Abraham Lincoln.)

Slavery and States' Rights

By the summer of 1860, the conflicts between North and South had become so explosive that it appeared the United States might soon be torn apart. In the previous ten years, presidents and Congress had struggled to find compromises between a growing movement in the North to restrict slavery and growing fears in the South that its way of life was being threatened.

On most of the issues that divided the two regions, Andrew Johnson stood with the South. He supported the Compromise of 1850. The compromise admitted California as a free state, which pleased antislavery supporters. At the same time, it included the Fugitive Slave Act, which supported slavery. The act committed the federal government to help catch runaway slaves in the North and return them to their owners in the South. In 1854, Johnson also supported the controversial Kansas-Nebraska Act, which provided that in these territories, residents would choose for themselves whether to permit or outlaw slavery. Soon afterward, proslavery and antislavery factions set up competing governments in Kansas and used intimidation and violence to gain the upper hand.

Johnson came from a region where there were no large plantations, and slavery was not an important part of the economy. During his political career he had been an outspoken opponent of wealthy plantation owners. Yet he believed that slavery was permitted by the Constitution, and he owned a few slaves himself. He believed, along with most southerners, in *states' rights*, the right of each

Slaves harvest cotton, the South's major crop, as a slave overseer and the plantation owner make conversation.

state to determine its own policies on slavery and other matters. He was deeply opposed to federal actions that limited or restricted states' rights.

Election and Secession

All these issues came together in the presidential election of 1860. Democratic president James Buchanan was retiring. At the Democratic nominating convention in 1860, the leading candidate was Senator Stephen Douglas of Illinois, who had been a major supporter of the Compromise of 1850 and had written the Kansas-Nebraska Act. Southern Democrats refused to support him, however. They walked out and nominated their own candidate, Vice President John C. Breckinridge of Kentucky.

The new Republican party had been established only a few years earlier. Its members strongly opposed the spread of slavery to new territories. The Republicans nominated a lawyer from Illinois named Abraham Lincoln. Lincoln had gained national attention in 1858 for a series of debates with Senator Douglas over the issue of slavery in the territories. In a famous speech, reprinted in newspapers around the country, he said, "A house divided against itself cannot stand," and predicted that the United States must one day permit slavery everywhere or nowhere.

The nomination of Lincoln caused widespread fear in the South. If he were elected, they believed, he and his Republican allies would restrict slavery and might abolish it altogether. With the Democratic party divided between two candidates, it seemed likely that Lincoln might win. Southerners began to talk about *seceding* from the Union—withdrawing from the United States to preserve states' rights and the system of slavery.

In the November election, Lincoln was victorious, and northern states elected many Republicans to the House and the Senate. Almost immediately, southern states called special conventions to discuss secession. Andrew Johnson agreed with his southern colleagues on many points, but on the issue of secession, he broke with them. To him the Constitution was written in stone and must never be tampered with or diminished in any way. Its opening words are "We the people of the United States . . . do ordain and establish this Constitution." This made it clear to him that the founding fathers considered the people, not the states, to be *sovereign*, or to possess the supreme authority. He believed a state had no legal right to secede.

After Lincoln's election, Johnson found that many of his friends and colleagues in Tennessee were talking about secession. He argued that the South could more effectively fight for its rights from inside rather than outside the framework of the Union. A Tennesseean asked, "What do you advise, Senator

Abraham Lincoln, who was elected president in 1860. Soon afterward in the Senate, Andrew Johnson condemned the southern states that were seceding from the Union.

Johnson, if Lincoln is elected?" Johnson's answer was clear and uncompromising. "I shall stay inside the Union and there fight for southern rights," he said. "I advise all others to do the same."

Six weeks after Lincoln's election, South Carolina became the first state to secede. On December 18, the senators from South Carolina stood up in the Senate and announced their resignations. As shouting erupted in the hall, Andrew Johnson pushed his way to the speaker's box and called out to be heard. When the noise died down, he said, "I am opposed to secession." The senators booed and cheered, but he refused to be shouted down. "I think that this battle ought to be fought not outside, but inside of the Union, and upon the battlements of the Constitution itself." He appealed to his colleagues' patriotism. He declared that he was unwilling "to walk outside of the Union which has been the result of a Constitution made by the patriots" who had fought the American Revolution. If the Constitution was good enough for Washington, Jefferson, and the other founding fathers, he thundered, "it is good enough for us."

Both Hated and Admired

When Johnson finished speaking, there was no applause. Instead, boos and insults flew from the Senate floor and the spectators' galleries above. Southern senators followed him to the cloakroom and then through the streets, taunting him, spitting at him, and challenging him to duels. Reports of the speech were transmitted throughout the country. In the South most people cursed Johnson and called him a traitor. He and his wife and children received numerous death threats.

In much of the North, Johnson was seen as a hero. The *New York Times* called him "the greatest man of the age," and thousands of letters of support flooded his office. The superintendent of the U.S. Census wrote, "Your praise is on all lips and I hear none speak of your noble and patriotic effort in the Senate but in terms of the highest commendation."

Johnson returned to Tennessee, where state leaders were considering secession. In January six more states seceded. Yet Johnson argued eloquently that Tennessee should not join them, and for a time he was successful. In March 1861, President Lincoln was inaugurated, and Tennessee remained in the Union. Then on April 12, forces from the secessionist states fired on Fort Sumter, a federal military post in the harbor of Charleston, South Carolina. President Lincoln declared a state of civil war and called for volunteers. The great Civil War had begun.

After Fort Sumter, even Andrew Johnson could not restrain his state from seceding from the Union. He still had some support in his own east Tennessee region, where many favored remaining in the Union, but the majority of Tennesseeans favored leaving the Union and joining the new Confederate States

When Confederates opened fire on Fort Sumter, South Carolina, in April 1861, the Civil War began. In June, Johnson's own state of Tennessee seceded, but Johnson refused to resign from the Senate and stayed in Washington.

of America. Johnson was in Washington when the state seceded. He was warned not to return to the state, and his wife and children were driven from their home in Greeneville.

By the summer of 1861, Andrew Johnson was the only remaining senator from a seceded state in the U.S. Senate. Even though his state had established a new government, he continued to pursue his duties. In July, working with Repre-sentative John J. Crittenden, he presented a resolution in the Senate seeking to define the aims of the Union in the war. It was a moderate statement, emphasizing that the single most important aim was to reestablish the Union under the U.S. Constitution.

Military Governor ———

By early 1862, Tennessee had become a major field of battle in the Civil War. In the western part of the state, General Ulysses S. Grant captured Confederate forts on the Tennessee and Cumberland Rivers in February. The loss of these important rivers forced the Confederates to give up Nashville. It was occupied by Union troops on February 23. President Lincoln, eager to dramatize the fall of a Confederate capital, asked Andrew Johnson to return to Tennessee and serve as military governor. He was to begin setting up a new Tennessee government loyal to the Union.

Fast Facts
THE CIVIL WAR

Who: The United States (the Union or the North) against the Confederate States of America, made up of southern states that had seceded from the Union.

When: April 12, 1861–May 1865

Why: Southern states, believing the election of Abraham Lincoln threatened states' rights and slavery, seceded from the United States and fought for their independence. The North fought to restore the southern states to the Union, and later to end slavery.

Where: States along the border between the Union and the Confederacy, especially Virginia and Tennessee. Confederate forces had some early successes, but were overcome by the Union's superior resources. Major northern victories came at Gettysburg, Pennsylvania, and Vicksburg, Mississippi (both July 1863); Atlanta, Georgia (September 1864); and Petersburg and Richmond, Virginia (both April 1865).

Outcome: The Confederate Army of Northern Virginia surrendered to Union forces April 9, 1865, ending the major fighting. The victorious North passed legislation that abolished slavery, gave civil rights to former slaves, and put defeated states under military rule. Efforts to reconstruct the South continued until 1877.

Not a War of Conquest

The War Aims Resolution was passed by the House of Representatives on July 22, 1861. On July 25, Johnson introduced it to the Senate, where it also passed. It helped set a moderate tone for the early period of the war and sought to reassure the citizens of the Confederate states. It begins by identifying secession of the southern states as the cause of the war, then continues:

> . . . that in this national emergency, Congress, banishing all feeling of mere passion or resentment, will recollect only its duty to the whole country; that this war is not prosecuted upon our part in any spirit of oppression, nor for any purpose of conquest or subjugation, nor for the purpose of overthrowing or interfering with the rights or established institutions of those States, but to defend and maintain the supremacy of the Constitution and all laws made in the pursuance thereof, and to preserve the Union, with all the dignity, equality, and rights of the several states unimpaired, and as soon as these objects are accomplished the war ought to cease.

☆ ★ ☆

Johnson accepted the appointment and headed for Nashville. He soon discovered, however, that much of the state was still under Confederate rule. Eastern Tennessee was occupied by Confederate troops, who would use it as a stepping-stone to attack Kentucky, even farther to the north. In the west, Memphis was still in Confederate hands as well. Johnson discovered that his job in Nashville was difficult enough. Many local leaders sympathized with the Confederacy and would have nothing to do with a new Union government. Johnson also found himself quarreling with leaders of the occupying Union army, who were not responsible to him. Johnson spoke out for the welfare of Tennessee citizens, but the Union army leaders thought first of their own troops.

Gradually, Union forces drove the Confederates out of Tennessee. In April, General Grant won a costly victory at Shiloh in the west, driving a large Confederate army south into Mississippi. In June, Union gunboats captured Memphis. In the eastern part of the state, however, Confederate armies were threatening Nashville itself. Finally, in January 1863, Union forces defeated a large Confederate army at Murfreesboro, only 40 miles (64 km) southwest of Nashville.

In the meantime, President Lincoln had been considering an emancipation proclamation, declaring all the slaves in the Confederate states to be free. Johnson opposed the proclamation. He warned Lincoln that it would reduce the support of Tennesseeans for the Union cause. He finally succeeded in excluding Tennessee from the proclamation. When the Emancipation Proclamation was issued, it did not free the slaves in Tennessee.

By 1864, Tennessee was under more secure Union control. Finally, Johnson's work to establish a new government began to take hold. Using persuasion when he could and his military powers when necessary, he had nearly put the government on its feet by the summer of 1864.

"Abe" and "Andy"

Republicans met in the summer of 1864 to nominate candidates for the presidential election in the fall. Lincoln would be running for reelection. Northern voters were tiring of the war, and the Republicans were worried that the president might not be reelected. As the party gathered for its nominating convention, one of the questions was who would be nominated for vice president. Lincoln's current vice president, Hannibal Hamlin, hoped to be nominated again, but Republican leaders were searching for a candidate who might contribute more to a winning campaign.

This would be the first presidential campaign in history to take place when the country was involved in a civil war, so Lincoln and Republican leaders agreed to run not as Republicans, but as a national Union party. This strategy focused attention on Andrew Johnson. He was a southerner and a Democrat who strongly supported the Union and had been contributing to the war effort. His nomination would deliver the message that Lincoln and his party welcomed all Union supporters, Republicans and Democrats. It would make a special point to voters in the slave states that remained in the Union, including Maryland, Delaware, Kentucky, and Missouri.

Lincoln himself made no public statements about choosing a nominee for vice president, claiming he wished to leave the choice to the delegates at the convention. However, he may have encouraged his own supporters to favor Johnson for the nomination. At the convention, Andrew Johnson won the vice presidential nomination.

Johnson's own Democratic party wrote a *platform* (a statement of political ideals and demands to be used in the campaign) that called for an early end to the war. They hoped to appeal to war-weary voters who preferred a compromise settlement instead of continued fighting. Then they nominated the most popular figure in the party, former general George B. McClellan, who had served as a leading general in the Union Army. McClellan said he would accept the nomination, but could not accept the part of the platform calling for an early end to the war.

During the campaign, political cartoonists had a field day. They showed "Abe" and "Andy," the rail-splitter and the tailor, working together to repair tears in the Union's fabric. They teased McClellan, a military professional, for running on a peace platform. Fortunately for the Republican-Union ticket, a Union army captured the important Confederate city of Atlanta only weeks before the

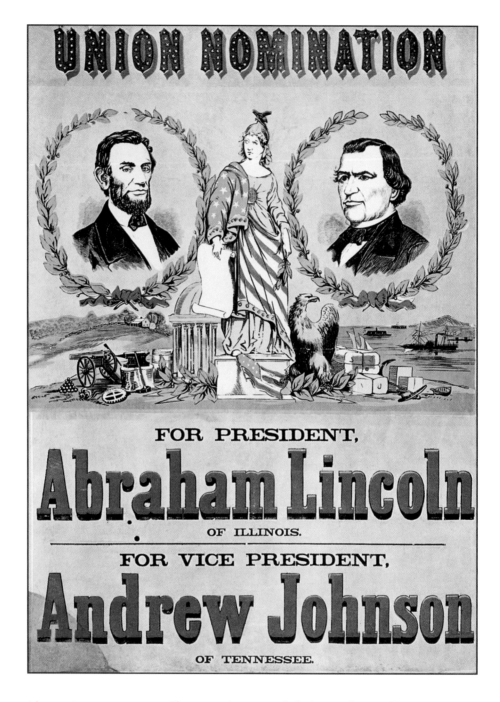

Johnson, a Democrat, was nominated for vice president to run with Abraham Lincoln, a Republican, in 1864. Republicans wanted to show their desire to bring the seceded states back into the Union and hoped to win the votes of Democrats in the border states.

election. Voters rallied to Lincoln and Johnson, and they carried nearly all the states in the Union, gaining 212 electoral votes to McClellan's 21.

Against all odds, Andrew Johnson, Democrat from Tennessee, had become vice president of the United States.

his audience. For several weeks afterward he did not appear in public, recovering from his fever and from his embarrassment.

Victory and Tragedy —————————————

In the weeks following the inauguration, the nation was swept along in a tide of momentous events. Early in April, the Union captured and occupied Richmond, Virginia, the capital of the Confederacy, forcing the Confederate government and the defending troops to flee. On April 9, Robert E. Lee, the proud commander of the Confederate army in Virginia, surrendered to Union general Ulysses S. Grant at Appomattox Courthouse, south of Richmond. This signaled the end of the long and bloody war between the states.

Church bells pealed throughout the Union states, and people poured into the streets celebrating the end of the war. The joy was short-lived, however. On the night of April 14, the vice president was asleep in his room at Kirkwood House, his residence in Washington. About 10:15 P.M., a loud knock on his door awakened him. "Governor Johnson!" came a frantic voice, "if you are in this room I must see you!"

Springing out of bed, Johnson opened his door. His friend, Leonard J. Farwell, former governor of Wisconsin, rushed into the room. President

An artist's conception of Abraham Lincoln's assassination on April 14, 1865, only six weeks after Lincoln and Johnson were inaugurated.

Lincoln had been shot by an assassin, Farwell told him. Johnson was so shaken by the news that he had to lean on his friend to keep from falling. Minutes later, armed guards arrived to protect the vice president in case assassins were after him, too.

Johnson was unable to sleep that night. At one point, a witness later recalled, he paced the floor and kept repeating the phrase: "They shall suffer for this," referring to the assassins. In the morning he received the news that Lincoln had died. Soon afterward, a messenger delivered a formal letter from Secretary of War Edwin M. Stanton and other members of Lincoln's cabinet:

> Sir: Abraham Lincoln, President of the United States, was shot by an assassin last evening at Ford's theater in this city and died at the hour of twenty-two minutes after seven o'clock [this morning]. . . . By the death of President Lincoln, the office of President has devolved [been handed down] under the Constitution upon you. The emergency of the government demands that you should immediately qualify, according to the requirements of the Constitution, and enter upon the duties of President of the United States. If you will please make known your pleasure, such arrangements as you deem proper will be made.

At 11 o'clock that morning, in the parlor of Kirkwood House, Johnson was sworn in as the 17th president. Supreme Court Chief Justice Salmon P. Chase administered the oath of office. Chase then told him, "You are president. May God support, guide, and bless you in your arduous labors." Thus began what would become one of the most difficult and turbulent presidencies in the history of the American Republic.

Johnson is sworn in as president on April 15 by Chief Justice of the Supreme Court Salmon Chase.

A Nation Still in Pieces

Johnson faced an awesome task. Much of the old Confederacy was in ruins. Normal business and commerce had come nearly to a stop. Many were hungry, and thousands of veterans were disabled or recovering from wounds. State governments loyal to the Confederacy were in shambles. In addition, there were four million African Americans in the Confederate states who had been freed from slavery by the terms of the Emancipation Proclamation and the 13th Amendment (which had been passed by Congress and was being ratified by the states). Now that they were freed, no longer provided with food and shelter by their masters, how would they make their livings? Most had no land of their own and no other property. Many were illiterate and had few skills. White citizens continued to believe that African Americans were inferior to whites. They did not accept that former slaves were now *freedmen* with basic human rights.

Citizens in the North were more prosperous. Few major battles had been fought in their territory, and business and commerce were flourishing. Yet they had suffered, too. Hundreds of thousands of young men had been killed or wounded during the war, leaving widows and orphans and mourning parents. Some were eager to see the Confederate states punished. Many others were determined to see that the huge sacrifices of the war would lead to real changes in the South. Northern political leaders spoke of the need to "reconstruct" the southern region with a new understanding of equality, enforced by new laws and regulations.

How could this Reconstruction be accomplished? Johnson knew that the question was being hotly debated even before he became president. President Lincoln and Congress had established Freedmen's Bureaus in regions occupied by Union forces to help slaves adjust to life as free men and women. These offices were already at work in the southern states. Yet Lincoln was caught up in a serious dispute with Congress about how to manage the southern states. He was in favor of encouraging their rapid reentry into the Union so that state government could be reestablished and states could elect representatives to the federal government.

One group of congressmen, known as the Radical Republicans, favored a much harsher plan. They believed it was impractical to set up new state governments in a few months. Instead, their plan called for military governments operated by Union troops until southern citizens agreed to reform their society and were willing to meet difficult standards for readmission to the Union.

Now this dispute was Andrew Johnson's problem. The Congress elected in 1862 had adjourned only days before Johnson became president. The new Congress, elected in 1864, was not scheduled to meet until December 1865. For

Andrew Johnson in a photograph taken soon after he became president.

seven and a half months, Johnson would have wide discretion to chart the course of Reconstruction. Congress would review his actions later, but he believed he could make great progress before they returned. Many citizens in the North and South were hoping that he could help put the nation back together.

The President's Plan

Johnson and his close advisers rapidly put together a plan, following the blueprint he believed that Lincoln favored. The main aim was to restore southern states to the Union as soon as possible, leaving many problems to be solved later. He appointed a provisional governor for each southern state and set out requirements for joining the Union. The state must write a new constitution, which must have certain provisions. First, it must accept the 13th Amendment to the Constitution, which *abolished*, or ended, slavery; and renounce the right of a state to secede from the Union.

A second provision was intended to restore residents of the southern states to citizenship. In May 1865, Johnson issued a blanket *amnesty*, or pardon, to most southerners who were willing to take an oath of loyalty to the Union and the Constitution. Certain groups did not qualify for the amnesty, including leaders of the Confederate government, former U.S. military officers who had fought for the Confederacy, and wealthy landowners and merchants who had actively

The States During the Presidency of Andrew Johnson

NEBRASKA
(1867)

☐ STATES WHEN PRESIDENT TOOK OFFICE
▨ JOINED UNION DURING PRESIDENCY (YEAR JOINED IN PARENTHESES)

supported the Confederate cause. People in these classes were required to apply directly to the president for a pardon. All who qualified for the amnesty or who had received a presidential pardon could run for office and could vote in elections for representatives to Congress.

Many southern leaders were relieved that Johnson's terms were so lenient. They began at once to draft constitutions and reestablish state governments under these guidelines. Thousands in the excluded classes wrote to Johnson or visited Washington in person to apply for pardons, and he granted pardons to nearly all who applied.

By the time Congress returned in December, all the Confederate states except Texas had submitted new constitutions for approval and had elected new members of Congress. To casual observers, it seemed that Johnson's Reconstruction plan might succeed in re-uniting the country in a matter of months. Those who looked more closely, however, saw dark clouds on the horizon.

The Missing Piece

Johnson's plan was curiously silent about one issue—the African American freedmen. He believed that any laws or regulations concerning the four million recently freed slaves should be written by the states. As a longtime believer in

First Lady Eliza McCardle Johnson. When her husband became president, Mrs. Johnson was ill with tuberculosis. She appeared in public only twice during his presidency. Several of the Johnsons' grown children lived in the White House, helping their parents both in public and in private.

states' rights, he felt that he was supported by the Constitution. Would they have the same rights as white citizens to move about freely, gain an education, own property, and carry on a business? Would they have voting rights? On these issues, his plan was silent.

Johnson recognized that former slaves were entitled to some rights. "Good faith requires the security of the freedmen in their liberty and personal property, their right to labor, and their right to claim the just return of their labor," he said. Yet he did not include any requirements of the southern states to assure that these rights were granted. He seemed to assume that the states could be trusted to make these regulations in "good faith."

Southern political leaders understood the situation differently. Since they were under no requirement to grant rights to former slaves, they did not. In fact, each state began making harsh new laws to govern the former slaves. In most states, African American freedmen were required to observe a curfew, forbidden to be out of their homes after dark. They were required to carry identification papers that included the name of the white employer for whom they worked. In some states, they were not allowed to own or rent property and could not hunt, fish, or graze their cattle on public lands. These "black codes" reduced freedmen to little more than slaves.

Congress Returns

When Congress returned in December, it moved quickly to express its disapproval of Johnson's Reconstruction program. Both houses refused to recognize or seat the new representatives from the southern states. Similarly, the new state constitutions were put aside for further review. The House and the Senate created a Joint Committee on Reconstruction and announced that all plans regarding organization and representation of southern states would have to be approved by the committee.

In February 1866, Congress passed a new bill enlarging the Freedmen's Bureau, the agency organized to provide help to newly freed slaves. The bureau offices in the South were staffed largely by northerners, including teachers, ministers, and former government officials. They provided food and shelter to former slaves displaced from their old homes and sought to provide basic education and help in finding land to farm or other employment. The bureau was deeply resented by white citizens. The bill also provided that southern whites accused of denying basic rights to freedmen could be tried by military tribunals.

When the Freedmen's Bureau Bill reached President Johnson's desk to be signed into law, he vetoed it. He sent a message to Congress suggesting that it was an illegal interference in the affairs of southern states. Three days later, on Washington's Birthday, he addressed a crowd of supporters outside the White

House. He said he had fought traitors and treason in the South during the war. Now that peace had come, he found himself facing a different group of troublesome men. These individuals, he said, were opposed to "the restoration of the Union of these states" and to "the fundamental principles of this government, and . . . are laboring to destroy it."

When some members of the crowd asked him to name three of these men, Johnson answered, "You ask me who they are? I say Thaddeus Stevens, of Pennsylvania, is one; I say Mr. Sumner, of the Senate, is another, and Wendell Phillips is another. . . . I do not intend to be overawed by real or pretended friends, nor do I intend to be bullied by my enemies. Honest conviction is my courage. The Constitution is my guide."

Johnson's veto and his angry accusations strengthened the hand of the Radical Republicans. They did not have the two-thirds majority in both houses to override his veto, but weeks later, they passed the Civil Rights Act, designed to force southern states to grant basic rights to former slaves. It defined all persons born in the United States (including former slaves) as citizens and listed some of the rights all citizens had. These included the right to own land, to make contracts (to buy or rent land, for example), and to "enjoy the full and equal benefit of all laws."

Once again, Johnson vetoed the bill, sticking to his belief in the right of individual states to deal with these issues. This time, Congress had the needed

As Republican Reconstruction took control of the South, more and more African Americans gained the right to vote.

votes to override his veto. In April, they voted by two-thirds majorities in both houses to make the Civil Rights Act law.

The disagreements between President Johnson and Congress had grown into a war. Johnson was defiant and refused to compromise on his principles. He seemed not to realize that he was losing not only the support of Congress, but also the support of Republican voters who had helped elect him. He believed he understood the problems and needs of the southern states, but he seemed not to understand at all the problems and needs of millions of former slaves or of political leaders in the North. This standoff between a president and Congress set the scene for one of the most contentious chapters in U.S. history.

Congressional Reconstruction ————

Seeing that no compromise with President Johnson was possible, Congress took matters into its own hands and began to create a Reconstruction program of its own. With the passage of the Civil Rights Act in April 1866, it saw that it had two-thirds majorities in both houses and could create the program without the president's approval.

That spring, Congressional leaders worked to create a new Constitutional amendment. Fearing that conservative judges might declare parts of the Civil Rights Act unconstitutional, they wanted to assure civil rights for all by making the provision part of the Constitution itself. They passed the 14th Amendment in June and sent it to the states for ratification. As part of their Reconstruction plan, they required southern states to ratify the amendment before they could send new representatives to Congress. President Johnson opposed the amendment, and encouraged states not to ratify it, but it was ratified by three-quarters of the states in July 1868.

The Election of 1866

Congressional elections in 1866 provided an opportunity for president and Congress to appeal to the people. Andrew Johnson worked to create a new party made up of conservative Republicans and Democrats. Republicans in Congress ran against Johnson and his refusal to work with Congress.

In August, Johnson set out on a speaking tour to campaign for candidates who supported his views. This was the first time a president had ever made such a campaign tour, and many political leaders believed that it cheapened the presidency. Worse yet, Johnson's outspoken style, which had won him great success in eastern Tennessee, made more enemies than friends. He described his opponents as traitors and accused Congress of dishonesty. In addition, he expressed strong opposition to giving full citizenship to former slaves in the South. Even Johnson's friends were embarrassed by his remarks.

The elections proved that Johnson had lost the debate. Republicans gained more than two-thirds of the seats in both houses of Congress, making it certain

Northern politicians, called "carpetbaggers" in the South, corrupted elections by offering money or other favors to African Americans if they would vote for Republicans.

that Congress would need to make no compromises with the president in the next two years.

Congress Acts

During this period of U.S. history, the Congress elected in November did not meet for the first time until the following December, more than a year later. The Congress elected in 1866, however, resolved to meet in March 1867, only one day after the previous Congress adjourned. They were ready to take on Andrew Johnson.

In a single day, they passed far-reaching legislation for reconstruction of the South. They divided the region into five military regions to be governed by northern officers. They set strict new rules for former Confederate states to meet before gaining readmission to the Union. Among these were that the state must ratify the 14th Amendment and that its constitution must give freedmen the right to vote.

Then Congress turned to the president. The Constitution provides that he shall be commander in chief of the armed forces, but Congress believed he would appoint military governors too sympathetic to southern whites. They passed a bill that required him to issue all military orders through the commanding general of the army, who at the time was Ulysses S. Grant. This assured that Johnson's appointments would require General Grant's approval.

Finally, the Congress passed the Tenure of Office Act. This restricted the president's power to dismiss or appoint members of his own cabinet without the prior approval of the Senate. Johnson's secretary of war, Edwin Stanton, openly supported the Radical Republicans in Congress. In fact, he was even reporting to them confidential conversations with Johnson. According to the new act, however, Johnson could not dismiss Stanton until he had chosen a replacement and gained the approval of the Senate.

The Radical Republicans

The Radical Republicans who took control of Congress in 1867 claimed to have the highest motives—to bring full citizenship and equal rights to former slaves in the South. Their opponents claimed that they had several less praiseworthy motives as well.

One of their major concerns was maintaining the power of the Republican party. They feared that if southern states rejoined the Union without allowing voting rights to freedmen, southern Democrats would be able to win majorities in Congress and perhaps even elect a president who opposed the end of slavery. They felt certain that former slaves would vote for Republicans. In fact, many workers in the Freedmen's Bureau were Republicans who encouraged freedmen to join the party and vote for Republicans.

A few of the Radicals may also have been seeking revenge. They believed that southern whites had caused untold suffering by starting the Civil War and deserved to be punished. They particularly despised former large plantation owners and proposed taking plantations from their owners to give to former slaves.

☆ ★ ☆

In September 1867, President Johnson issued a new and more sweeping amnesty, pardoning additional southern whites. He hoped that the pardons would help moderate congressional Reconstruction, but they had little immediate effect.

Edwin Stanton, who was secretary of war when Johnson became president, reported to Johnson's enemies in Congress on his actions and conversations. Congress passed the Tenure of Office Act, which forbade the president to dismiss Stanton and other high government officials unless Congress agreed.

Stanton's Treachery —

Edwin Stanton had served as Abraham Lincoln's secretary of war through much of the Civil War and was kept on by Johnson after he became president. By 1867, Stanton openly supported the Radical Republicans in Congress, and by terms of the Tenure of Office Act, Johnson could not dismiss him. He learned in 1867 that Stanton was reporting regularly to Congress even on private White House matters.

Johnson also learned that Stanton had purposely misled him about evidence against Mary Surratt, who had been con-

The newly appointed secretary of war, General Lorenzo Thomas (left), demands that Stanton give up his office. Stanton refused. Three days later, the U.S. House of Representatives voted to impeach President Johnson for firing Stanton.

victed of taking part in the plot to kill Lincoln. The military court found reasonable doubt about her guilt and recommended that her death sentence be commuted. Stanton never reported this recommendation to the president, and Mary Surratt was executed. Johnson exclaimed, "To think that the man I trusted was plotting and intriguing against me!"

On August 5, 1867, Johnson demanded that Stanton resign. Stanton refused. "It is impossible to get along with such a man in such a position, and I can stand it no longer," Johnson said. He suspended Stanton on August 12 and appointed General Grant in his place. Congress was not in session, so it could not object.

In January 1868, after Congress convened again, it rejected Johnson's reasons for suspending Stanton and ordered that Stanton be reinstated. Johnson reluctantly agreed. Then on February 21, he openly defied Congress by dismissing Stanton and appointing General Lorenzo Thomas his new secretary of war. Stanton refused to leave his office, barricading the door. Three days later, the House of Representatives voted to *impeach* Andrew Johnson, accusing him of "high crimes and misdemeanors" and hoping to convict him and remove him from office.

Chapter 5

The House Brings Charges ——————

The battle between President Johnson and Congress had become more than a disagreement about Reconstruction policy. Now it was also a battle between two branches of the federal government. The writers of the Constitution intended that the legislative branch (Congress) should make laws and the executive branch (the president) should enforce them. Now, however, Congress was making *and* enforcing the Reconstruction laws. Congress had also taken control of the country's military forces, even though the Constitution designates the president as commander in chief. It also had restricted the president's power to appoint officers in the executive branch. Andrew Johnson had been stripped of his power, and the presidency itself had been weakened.

The day after voting to impeach Andrew Johnson, the House impeachment managers, led by Thaddeus Stevens of Pennsylvania

Congressman Thaddeus Stevens of Pennsylvania was a leader of the movement to impeach Johnson. Here he is reading the finished Articles of Impeachment to members of the House.

and John A. Bingham of Ohio, delivered the official notification of impeachment to the Senate. In the days that followed, the House impeachment managers drew up a list of eleven charges against the president.

Following the procedures outlined in the Constitution, the House impeachment managers would serve as the prosecutors, the Chief Justice of the United States would preside as the judge, and the Senate would hear the case as the jury. In order to convict the president on any charge, two-thirds of the senators would have to vote him guilty. If Johnson was convicted of any charge, he would be removed from office.

On March 7, the clerk of the Senate visited the White House and delivered the official summons to Johnson, listing the eleven charges against him. The three main charges were that he had violated the Tenure of Office Act by firing Secretary Stanton; that he had defamed Congress in his public speeches; and that he had tried to stop Congress from doing its job.

Johnson Reacts

In an interview with a reporter from the *New York World*, Johnson responded to at least one of the charges publicly. He denied that he had defamed or injured Congress, saying,

What does the Constitution say? It says: "The President . . . shall be removed from office on impeachment for and conviction of treason, bribery, or other high crimes and misdemeanors.". . . Is telling the truth to the American people in a public address a "high misdemeanor"? . . . I have advised Congress directly, and many times, of . . . its unwise, unconstitutional, and disastrous legislation. If I have advised the people of it in terms not exactly befitting a state document, it is because the more pointedly the truth is told, the quicker the masses of the people apprehend it.

☆ ★ ☆

HARPER'S WEEKLY

A JOURNAL OF CIVILIZATION.

VOL. XII.—No. 587.]   NEW YORK, SATURDAY, MARCH 28, 1868.   [SINGLE COPIES, TEN CENTS. $4.00 PER YEAR IN ADVANCE.

Entered according to Act of Congress, in the Year 1868, by Harper & Brothers, in the Clerk's Office of the District Court of the United States, for the Southern District of New York.

The sergeant at arms of the Senate informs President Johnson that he will be tried for "high crimes and misdemeanors" in an impeachment trial.

On March 13, the president's lawyers asked for 40 days to prepare the case, not a long time considering the serious nature of the charges. The Radical Republican leaders denied the request. Impeachment manager Benjamin Butler argued that the case should be tried immediately. One of Johnson's attorneys argued that it was unfair and improper to deal with so important a matter "with railroad speed."

"Why not?" Butler answered. "Railroads have affected all other business, [so] why not trials?"

The chief justice finally settled the matter by allowing ten days for the president's defense to prepare. The trial itself finally got underway on March 30.

The Trial

The trial began on March 30 with opening arguments. Congressman Thaddeus Stevens of Pennsylvania, a longtime critic of Johnson and a leader of the impeachment movement, was too ill to serve as chief prosecutor, so the task fell to Congressman Benjamin Butler of Massachusetts. The prosecution focused on Johnson's action in firing Secretary of War Stanton, violating the Tenure of Office Act. The managers of the prosecution believed that this act was most likely to succeed in convicting the president.

The committee on impeachment in the House. Thaddeus Stevens is second from the left in the front row. These men became the prosecutors who presented the case against Johnson in the impeachment trial.

Johnson's defense attorneys replied that he had dismissed Stanton, but that he was within his rights to do so. Even if his actions violated the Tenure of Office Act, they could not be considered "treason, bribery, or other high crimes or misdemeanors," in the words of the Constitution.

President Johnson meets with his lawyers to prepare their case for the defense.

In the following weeks, the prosecutors presented documentary evidence, then called witnesses testifying to the president's actions and to the speeches he had given that defamed or ridiculed the Congress. The defense case was much shorter, and called only two witnesses.

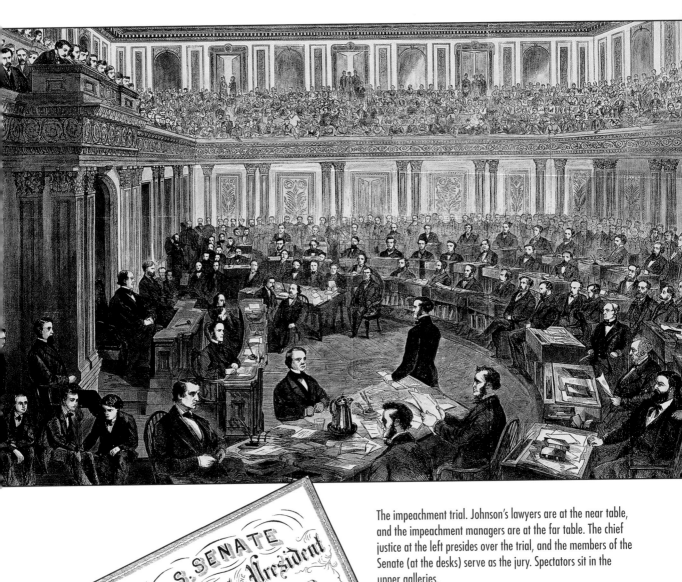

The impeachment trial. Johnson's lawyers are at the near table, and the impeachment managers are at the far table. The chief justice at the left presides over the trial, and the members of the Senate (at the desks) serve as the jury. Spectators sit in the upper galleries.

U. S. SENATE
Impeachment OF THE *President*
ADMIT THE BEARER
MARCH 13, 1868
Geo. T. Brown
Sergeant-at-Arms.

To be taken up at MAIN ENTRANCE
U. S. SENATE
No.
U. S. SENATE
Philp & Solomons, Wash. D.C.

A ticket admitting one person to attend the impeachment trial as a spectator.

Johnson's chief lawyer, Henry Stanbery, insisted that Johnson not attend the trial in person. He considered it below the president's dignity to be present at the proceedings, and he may have feared that Johnson might insist on speaking out. Johnson's blunt and tactless speech could damage his case and might even result in conviction. Johnson agreed with his lawyer's advice and attended none of the trial sessions.

When the trial was over, the Senate discussed the case privately. Finally, on May 16, they gathered to vote on the eleventh article of impeachment, which rolled all the charges into one. It was clear that a majority would vote "guilty," but no one knew if two-thirds of the senators would do so. The chief justice asked one senator after another, "How say you, guilty or not guilty?" Spectators kept score of the vote, trying to guess how it would come out. When all had voted, the clerk announced the result. Of the 54 senators, 35 voted "guilty," and 19 voted "not guilty." The "guilty" votes were one vote short of a two-thirds majority.

The Senate adjourned for ten days. Then it met one final time to vote on other articles of impeachment. On each of the votes, the result was exactly the same, 35 to 19. The president had been acquitted by the narrowest possible margin. He would not be removed from office.

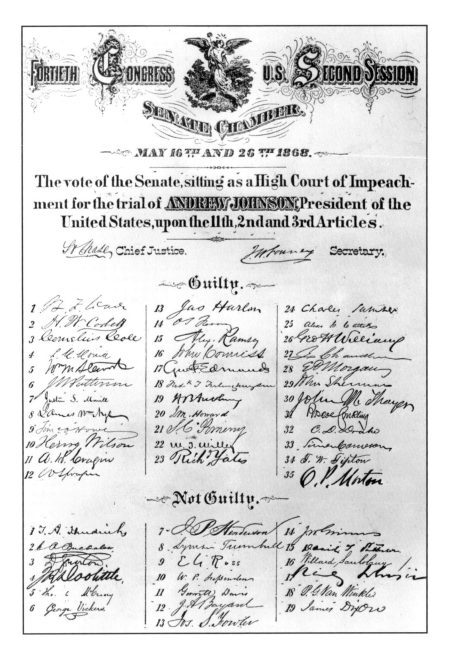

The verdict. The Senate voted 35 "guilty" and 19 "not guilty," one short of the required two-thirds majority. Johnson was therefore found not guilty, and he remained in office until the end of his term.

Explaining the Vote

It was clear that the Republicans opposing Johnson had a two-thirds majority in the Senate to pass Reconstruction legislation. Then why did they not convict Johnson and remove him from office? There were many explanations.

Some senators may have been convinced by the defense argument that Johnson's actions did not meet the standards set by the Constitution for impeachment. Not even the prosecutors claimed he was guilty of treason or bribery. The question was whether removing Edwin Stanton as secretary of war could be called a "high crime or misdemeanor."

Many Republicans believed that the prosecution's case had been badly handled. The chief prosecutor, Benjamin Butler, was a proud and self-important man. He was better known for his exploits as a general during the Civil War than for his skill as a prosecutor. His closing arguments embarrassed even his own supporters and may have lost important votes in the Senate.

Others in the Senate were worried about the practical effects of Johnson's impeachment. If Johnson were removed from office, there was no vice president to take his place. According to the Constitution, the office would go to the president pro tem (the elected chairman) of the Senate, Benjamin Wade. Wade was among the most radical of Radical Republicans, and many, even in his own party, were not comfortable putting him in the presidency. In addition, Johnson's term of office was coming to an end. Presidential elections were only six months away, and Johnson would surely not be elected to a full term. Some senators may have decided to let the voters decide who the next president should be.

Finally, some senators took a longer view. Republican Lyman Trumbull of Illinois was one of seven Republican senators who voted "not guilty." After the trial, he explained his vote:

> Once set the example of impeaching a President for what, when the excitement of the hour shall have subsided, will be regarded as insufficient causes . . . and no future President will be safe who happens to differ with a majority of the House and two thirds of the Senate on any measure deemed by them important, particularly if of a political character.

Trumbull did not believe that Johnson had been an effective president, and he disagreed with him about many things. Yet he believed that Congress should not impeach a president simply because he was outspoken or because it disagreed with his views.

Mixed Responses to the Verdict —————————

Many reactions to Johnson's acquittal were loud and emotional. Hearing the results of the vote, Thaddeus Stevens, one of the impeachment managers, waved his arms in the air and shouted, "The country is going to the devil!"

Those who were working in the South to root out the old slavery mentality and prepare freedmen for citizenship were depressed and bitter. They believed that Johnson's acquittal would delay the day when a new and different South could arise. "It is with sadness we learn that the greatest traitor of the century is acquitted," wrote one Florida Republican.

Other reactions were more positive. Johnson received many letters of congratulation from supporters. One said, "Permit me to mingle my heartiest congratulations with those of the tens of thousands of my fellow citizens who are doubtless, at this moment, offering you theirs, of the grand result yesterday of the great State Trial at Washington. . . . I find it impossible, as an American citizen, adequately to convey to you my gratification at the result."

Last Days as President —————————

Johnson himself was overjoyed by the verdict, yet he knew that he was still surrounded by determined opponents. The Congress still had the upper hand, and he

THIS LITTLE BOY WOULD PERSIST IN HANDLING BOOKS ABOVE HIS CAPACITY.

AND THIS WAS THE DISASTROUS RESULT.

Radical magazines ridiculed Johnson. In this cartoon, he is a little boy who is crushed by a big book called "Constitution of U.S."

would have little or no power to affect events during the remaining months of his presidency. A majority of the Senate and a majority of Americans still believed that he had performed poorly as president.

The truth of this observation was brought home soon afterward. Six weeks after the close of the trial, the Democrats met in New York City to choose a candidate for president in the upcoming national election. Johnson had let his supporters know that he would be happy to receive the nomination. He believed

Defiant to the End

Although nearly powerless as president and wounded by the attacks of his powerful opponents, Johnson never lost the belief that he had been in the right. He had harsh words for his Republican opponents, calling them "pretended patriots."

In his final days in office, he wrote out a "Farewell Address," which was published in newspapers and pamphlets throughout the country. Reviewing his presidency, he wrote,

> I feel that, with a sense of accountability to God, having conscientiously endeavored to discharge my whole duty, I have nothing to regret. Events have proved the correctness of [my policies]. . . . It is a matter of pride and gratification, in retiring from the most exalted position in the gift of a free people, to feel and know that in a long, arduous, and eventful public life, my action has never been influenced by desire for gain. . . . No responsibility for wars that have been waged . . . rests upon me. My thoughts have been those of peace.

In the address, he even included a parting shot at the Radical Republicans who had made his administration one of the most unhappy in history:

> [These men] have consistently sought to . . . retard the restoration of peace and harmony, and, by every means, to keep open and exposed to the poisonous breath of party passion the terrible wounds of a four-years' war. . . . They have . . . conspired to change the system of our government. . . . It will also be recorded as one of the marvels of the times that a party claiming for itself a monopoly of . . . patriotism . . . endeavored, by a costly and deliberate trial, to impeach one who defended the Constitution and the Union . . . during his whole term of office.

that a revived Democratic party under his leadership could turn the country toward a gentler and more just policy in the South. He received 65 votes on the first ballot, but the convention never really favored Johnson, who had been damaged by his long battle with Congress and by his impeachment. The convention nominated the governor of New York, Horatio Seymour.

The Republicans, on whose ticket Johnson had been elected vice president only four years earlier, had no interest at all in nominating Johnson. Their convention was controlled by the Republicans in Congress who had been at war with Johnson for the past three years. They nominated General Ulysses S. Grant, who had served Johnson as general of the army and briefly as acting secretary of war. Because of his contribution to the Union's victory in the Civil War, he was the most popular figure in the nation. He defeated Seymour easily and would serve as president for the next eight years.

Chapter 6

Remembering the Good ——————

Andrew Johnson's presidency had been so turbulent that some of his achievements were nearly forgotten. Perhaps the most important accomplishment of his administration was the purchase of Alaska. During the constant battles over Reconstruction, Johnson's secretary of state, William Seward, was ably handling the foreign and diplomatic affairs of the country. When he reported that the Russian czar might be willing to sell Alaska, Johnson supported him enthusiastically. Seward negotiated the purchase, but Congress, seeking to obstruct Johnson in every area, refused to approve the money for the deal. Johnson and Seward outmaneuvered Congress by persuading the Russians to accept the money later than the treaty called for. Critics of the purchase called Alaska "Seward's Folly" and "Johnson's Polar Bear Garden." Nearly a hundred years later, it

William Seward, who served as secretary of state to presidents Lincoln and Johnson. He negotiated the purchase of Alaska from the Russian government, one of the few successful actions while Johnson was president.

became the 49th state. If Johnson had not acted boldly when he did, Alaska would likely have become a possession of Britain or Canada.

Return Home

The Johnson family returned to a bittersweet welcome in Greeneville. Across the main street stretched a huge banner with the words "Welcome Home, Andrew Johnson, Patriot." After giving a short speech to a large crowd of well-wishers, Johnson retired with Eliza Johnson to the family's brick house. Although his daughter Mary had recently cleaned it up, the house had been damaged by both Confederate and Union soldiers during the war, and many of the family's possessions had been lost.

Memory of a Lost Book

Among the losses was Johnson's collection of books. "I regret the loss of my books," he told a reporter. "They were not valuable in one sense of the word, but dollars and cents cannot replace them. There was one in particular that I believe formed a turning point in my life. . . . This book was a volume of extracts from the speeches of Pitt, Fox, Burke, and other English orators. . . . How many times I have read the book I am unable to say, but I am satisfied . . . it . . . caused my life to take a different turn from what it otherwise would."

☆ ☆ ☆

Johnson was home, but he refused to retire. He immediately began campaigning to win election once again to the U.S. Senate. In his mind there were terrible wrongs to be righted back in Washington. If he could not address them as president, he would do so within the very Congress that had tried to ruin him.

His new campaign was an uphill battle. Tennessee had been readmitted into the Union less than three years before, in July 1866. The state was still wracked by bitterness and violence. Many remembered that Johnson himself had been military governor of the state during the war. Under the new Republican government, African Americans had the right to vote, but often the Ku Klux Klan and other secret societies used threats and violence to keep them away from the polls.

Once again, Johnson tried to take the middle ground. He did not think that most African Americans were ready to vote or hold public office. Yet he opposed the hatred and violence advocated by the Klan. "The Radical Congress made a serious blunder when they enfranchised the Negro race as a whole," he said. "But let bygones be bygones and let us live together in peace and good fellowship." This moderate stance hurt Johnson. Radicals condemned him for not supporting equality for former slaves. Conservatives felt he was far too nice to both blacks and radicals. So he failed to win election to the Senate.

Andrew Johnson late in his presidency.

For the next three years Johnson kept a close watch on Tennessee politics, waiting for another opportunity. His persistence paid off. In January 1875 he ran for the Senate again and this time was elected. He was the only former president to serve as a U.S. senator after leaving the White House. News of his victory stunned the nation. One newspaper called it "the most magnificent personal triumph which the history of American politics can show." Another declared, "No common man could have dug himself out of a pit so deep and so dark as that into which he had fallen." On March 5, Johnson proudly took his seat in the Senate. And on March 22 he rose and delivered a rousing speech criticizing the widespread corruption in President Grant's administration.

Illness and Death

Johnson had plans to become an influential leader in Washington once again, but then illness intervened. In July 1875, he traveled to Carter County, Tennessee, to visit his daughter Mary. Eliza Johnson had arrived there a few days earlier for the brief family reunion. On July 29, according to the Greeneville *Intelligencer*:

> Shortly after dinner he retired to his room upstairs, followed by one
>
> of his granddaughters, Miss Lillie Stover. She was engaged in
>
> conversation with him, he sitting in an armchair and she standing near.

Something outside called her attention to the window for a moment, when she heard her grandfather fall to the floor. She turned to him and in alarm called for help. They came and found the senator lying upon the carpet helpless.

Johnson had suffered a stroke. The next day, he had another stroke and fell into a coma, from which he did not wake. A few hours later, early in the morning of July 31, surrounded by family members, Andrew Johnson died.

Johnson had desired no religious ceremonies at his funeral. Following his wishes, he was placed in his coffin with a copy of the Constitution beneath his head and a U.S. flag draped around his body. A plate on the coffin bore the inscription "Andrew Johnson, Seventeenth President of the United States." On August 2, Johnson's body lay in state for a few hours in an assembly hall in Greeneville. Then, as a band played a solemn funeral march, a massive crowd of mourners half a mile long bore him to the gravesite on a nearby hill.

Johnson's Legacy

Andrew Johnson rose from poverty through energy, courage, and political talent. During the 1860s, his brave defense of the Union made him an enemy in his home region, but also made him many friends and supporters. He was nominated

This bronze statue of Andrew Johnson stands in his hometown of Greeneville, Tennessee.

and elected vice president because he represented the strong will of the nation to restore the Union after four years of war. Then he became president through the death of the Union's wartime leader.

The entrance to the Andrew Johnson National Cemetery, where the 17th president is buried.

The monument that stands over Andrew Johnson's gravesite.

Johnson inherited a country still at war with itself. Anger and hatreds threatened the peace in North and South alike. Johnson struggled to bring the Union back together. He was confident that he knew the right path, but his political instincts failed him. His opponents in Congress were equally sure they were right, and they defeated him at every turn. Johnson and his opponents were never able to talk with each other or cooperate to reunite the country. Johnson never achieved his vision for the Union, and he left the presidency much weaker than he found it. He remained confident and defiant to the end of his life, but he may also have understood he had failed to realize his greatest dreams for his country.

Fast Facts
Andrew Johnson

Birth:	December 29, 1808
Birthplace:	Raleigh, North Carolina
Parents:	Jacob and Mary McDonough Johnson
Brothers & Sisters:	William (born 1804); Elizabeth (1806–1807?)
Education:	Largely self-taught
Occupation:	Tailor, public official
Marriage:	To Eliza McCardle, May 17, 1827
Children:	(see First Lady Fast Facts, next page)
Political Parties:	Democratic (to 1864, 1869–1875); Union party (1864–1869)
Government Service:	1830–1836 Alderman, Greeneville, Tennessee
	1835–1841 Tennessee State Legislature
	1841–1843 Tennessee State Senate
	1843–1853 U.S. House of Representatives
	1853–1857 Governor of Tennessee
	1857–1862 U.S. Senate
	1862–1865 Military Governor of Tennessee
	1865 Vice President of the United States
	1865–1869 17th President of the United States
	1875 U.S. Senate
His Vice President:	None
Major Actions as President:	1865, May Issues first amnesty to former Confederates
	1865 Supports readmission of Confederate states, Congress refuses to recognize
	1866 Vetoes Freedmen's Bureau Act, Civil Rights Act; Congress overrides
	1867 Vetoes military reconstruction acts, Tenure of Office Act; Congress overrides
	1867 Approves purchase of Alaska from Russia
	1868, Feb., Dismisses Secretary of War Stanton, House votes impeachment
	1868, May, Johnson acquitted after impeachment trial
Firsts:	First president to be impeached
Death:	July 31, 1875, in Carter's Station, Tennessee
Age at Death:	66 years
Burial Place:	Andrew Johnson National Cemetery, Greeneville, Tennessee

Fast Facts Eliza McCardle Johnson

Birth:	October 4, 1810
Birthplace:	Greeneville, Tennessee
Parents:	John and Sarah Phillips McCardle
Brothers & Sisters:	None
Education:	Rhea Academy, Greeneville, Tennessee
Marriage:	To Andrew Johnson, May 17, 1827
Children:	Martha (1828–1901)
	Charles (1830–1863)
	Mary (1832–1883)
	Robert (1834–1869)
	Andrew Jr. (1852–1879)
Death:	January 15, 1876
Age at Death:	65 years
Burial Place:	Andrew Johnson National Cemetery, Greeneville, Tennessee

Timeline

1808	1818	1824	1826	1827
Andrew Johnson born at Raleigh, North Carolina, December 29.	Becomes an apprentice in the tailor shop of J. J. Selby.	Escapes from apprenticeship with his brother.	Johnson family moves to Greeneville, Tennessee.	Johnson opens a tailor shop in Greeneville; marries Eliza McCardle, May 17.

1853	1857	1860	1860	1861
Elected governor of Tennessee; serves to 1857.	Elected to the U.S. Senate; serves to 1862.	Helps pass Homestead Act in Congress; bill is vetoed by President Buchanan.	Abraham Lincoln elected president, November; South Carolina secedes from the United States, December; Johnson defends the Union in Senate speech, December 18.	The Civil War begins, April; Tennessee secedes from the Union, June; Johnson remains in Senate, sponsors a conciliatory War Aims Resolution, July.

1867	1867	1868	1868	1869
Vetoes first Military Reconstruction Act and Tenure of Office Act, March; Congress passes both bills over his vetoes.	Johnson issues second amnesty proclamation, September.	Johnson dismisses Secretary of War Stanton, February 21; House votes to impeach Johnson, February 24; after trial, Johnson acquitted by one vote, May 16 and May 26.	Ulysses S. Grant elected president, November.	Johnson publishes farewell address and leaves Washington, March.

1829

Elected alderman in Greeneville, serves 1830-1836; twice elected mayor by the board of aldermen.

1835

Elected to Tennessee state legislature, serves until 1841.

1841

Elected to the state senate, serves to 1843.

1842

Elected to U.S. House of Representatives, representing Tennessee's First District; serves 1843–1853.

1846

Proposes a homestead act in Congress, to grant government land to small farmers.

1862

President Lincoln appoints Johnson military governor of Tennessee.

1864

Johnson nominated to run as Lincoln's vice president on Union party ticket; Lincoln and Johnson are elected, November.

1865

Lincoln and Johnson inaugurated, March; Lee's Confederate Army surrenders, April 9; Lincoln shot, April 14; Lincoln dies and Johnson sworn in as president, April 15.

1865

Johnson issues amnesty proclamation, offering pardon to former Confederates, July 29; Congress refuses to seat members elected by former Confederate states, December.

1866

Johnson vetoes the Freedmen's Bureau Bill and Civil Rights Act; Congress overrides vetoes.

1869

Defeated for election to the U.S. Senate from Tennessee, October.

1875

Elected to the Senate from Tennessee, January; delivers first speech to the Senate, March; dies July 31 after a brief illness.

Glossary

abolish: to end; the 13th Amendment to the Constitution abolished slavery

amnesty: an official action pardoning an individual or group for past actions

freedmen: former slaves

impeach: under the U.S. Constitution, to charge a high official with misconduct; if convicted, the official is removed from office

platform: a party's statement of political ideals and demands used in an election campaign

secede: to withdraw from a government; the southern states seceded from the United States in 1861

sovereign: possessing supreme authority; able to act without approval of a higher authority

states' rights: in the 1800s, the view that each state in the United States had the right to make its own laws without review or interference by the federal government

veto: in the U.S. government, the president's refusal to sign a bill passed by Congress into law; Congress may *override* a veto by passing the bill by two-thirds majorities in both the House and the Senate

Further Reading

Dubowski, Cathy E. *Andrew Johnson: Rebuilding the Union*. Westwood, NJ: Silver
Burdette, 1991.

Harper, Judith E. *Andrew Johnson: Our Seventeenth President*. Chanhaussen, MN:
Child's World, 2002.

Malone, Mary. *Andrew Johnson*. Berkeley Heights, NJ: Enslow, 1999.

Naden, Corinne J. *Civil War Ends: Assassination, Reconstruction, and the Aftermath*.
New York: Raintree Steck-Vaughn, 2000.

Nardo, Don. *The U.S. Congress*. San Diego: Lucent Books, 1994.

——, *The U.S. Presidency*. San Diego: Lucent Books, 1995.

Stevens, Rita. *Andrew Johnson: 17th President of the U.S.* Deerfield Beach, FL: Garrett,
1989.

MORE ADVANCED READING

Hearn, Chester G. *The Impeachment of Andrew Johnson*. Jefferson, NC: McFarland,
2000.

Trefousse, Hans L. *Andrew Johnson: A Biography*. New York: Norton, 1989.

——, *Impeachment of a President*. Knoxville: University of Tennessee Press, 1975.

Places to Visit

★ ★ ★ ★ ★

Andrew Johnson Museum and Library
P.O. Box 5026
Greeneville, TN 37743
(423) 636-7348 or 1-800-729-0256

Located on the campus of Tusculum
College, in Greeneville, Tennessee, the
museum contains artifacts relating to
Johnson's life and times; the library offers
a collection of many letters, speeches, and
other important papers. For hours and
directions, see
http://ajmuseum.tusculum.edu

Andrew Johnson National Historic Site
121 Monument Avenue
Greeneville, TN 37743-5552
Visitor Information: (423) 638-3551

Also located in Greeneville, Johnson's
permanent home. The site includes his
two homes, his tailor shop, and his grave.
For more information, see
http://www.nps.gov/anjo

White House
1600 Pennsylvania Avenue NW
Washington, DC 20500
Visitors' Office: (202) 456-7041

Johnson's home from 1865 to 1869. For
more information, visit the White House
Web site (see next page).

Online Sites of Interest

★ **Internet Public Library, Presidents of the United States (IPL POTUS)**

http://www.ipl.org/div/potus/ajohnson.html

Includes concise information about Johnson and his presidency and useful links to other Internet sites. Operated by the School of Information at the University of Michgan.

★ **americanpresident.org**

http://www.americanpresident.org/history/andrewjohnson

An opening thumbnail biography is supported by pages with more detailed information on Johnson's early life, political career, and presidency. The site is operated by the Miller Center at the University of Virginia.

★ **The White House**

http://www.whitehouse.gov/history/presidents/aj17.html

A general overview of Johnson's life and deeds, compiled and presented by the White House in Washington, D.C. Similar information about all of the U.S. presidents, their wives, and many other important historical figures is also available at this useful site.

★ **The Civil War and Reconstruction, 1861–1877**

http://memory.loc.gov/ammem/ndlpedu/features/timeline/civilwar/civilwar.html

This excellent site provided by the Library of Congress offers an overview of the war and the programs instituted to reconstruct the South after the conflict. Contains several links to sites with related information.

★ **The Impeachment of Andrew Johnson**

http://www.impeach-andrewjohnson.com

Harper's Weekly provides this extremely informative site that gives a comprehensive overview of the trial, along with short biographies of all the major figures involved, including Thaddeus Stevens and the other congressional radicals. Highly recommended.

Table of Presidents

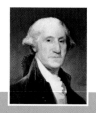  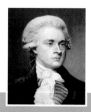 

1. George Washington   **2. John Adams**   **3. Thomas Jefferson**   **4. James Madison**

	1. George Washington	2. John Adams	3. Thomas Jefferson	4. James Madison
Took office	Apr 30 1789	Mar 4 1797	Mar 4 1801	Mar 4 1809
Left office	Mar 3 1797	Mar 3 1801	Mar 3 1809	Mar 3 1817
Birthplace	Westmoreland Co, VA	Braintree, MA	Shadwell, VA	Port Conway, VA
Birth date	Feb 22 1732	Oct 20 1735	Apr 13 1743	Mar 16 1751
Death date	Dec 14 1799	July 4 1826	July 4 1826	June 28 1836

9. William H. Harrison   **10. John Tyler**   **11. James K. Polk**   **12. Zachary Taylor**

	9. William H. Harrison	10. John Tyler	11. James K. Polk	12. Zachary Taylor
Took office	Mar 4 1841	Apr 6 1841	Mar 4 1845	Mar 5 1849
Left office	**Apr 4 1841•**	Mar 3 1845	Mar 3 1849	**July 9 1850•**
Birthplace	Berkeley, VA	Greenway, VA	Mecklenburg Co, NC	Barboursville, VA
Birth date	Feb 9 1773	Mar 29 1790	Nov 2 1795	Nov 24 1784
Death date	Apr 4 1841	Jan 18 1862	June 15 1849	July 9 1850

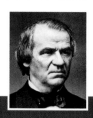  

17. Andrew Johnson   **18. Ulysses S. Grant**   **19. Rutherford B. Hayes**   **20. James A. Garfield**

	17. Andrew Johnson	18. Ulysses S. Grant	19. Rutherford B. Hayes	20. James A. Garfield
Took office	Apr 15 1865	Mar 4 1869	Mar 5 1877	Mar 4 1881
Left office	Mar 3 1869	Mar 3 1877	Mar 3 1881	**Sept 19 1881•**
Birthplace	Raleigh, NC	Point Pleasant, OH	Delaware, OH	Orange, OH
Birth date	Dec 29 1808	Apr 27 1822	Oct 4 1822	Nov 19 1831
Death date	July 31 1875	July 23 1885	Jan 17 1893	Sept 19 1881

5. James Monroe

Mar 4 1817

Mar 3 1825

Westmoreland Co, VA

Apr 28 1758

July 4 1831

6. John Quincy Adams

Mar 4 1825

Mar 3 1829

Braintree, MA

July 11 1767

Feb 23 1848

7. Andrew Jackson

Mar 4 1829

Mar 3 1837

The Waxhaws, SC

Mar 15 1767

June 8 1845

8. Martin Van Buren

Mar 4 1837

Mar 3 1841

Kinderhook, NY

Dec 5 1782

July 24 1862

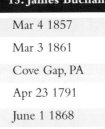

13. Millard Fillmore

July 9 1850

Mar 3 1853

Locke Township, NY

Jan 7 1800

Mar 8 1874

14. Franklin Pierce

Mar 4 1853

Mar 3 1857

Hillsborough, NH

Nov 23 1804

Oct 8 1869

15. James Buchanan

Mar 4 1857

Mar 3 1861

Cove Gap, PA

Apr 23 1791

June 1 1868

16. Abraham Lincoln

Mar 4 1861

Apr 15 1865•

Hardin Co, KY

Feb 12 1809

Apr 15 1865

21. Chester A. Arthur

Sept 19 1881

Mar 3 1885

Fairfield, VT

Oct 5 1830

Nov 18 1886

22. Grover Cleveland

Mar 4 1885

Mar 3 1889

Caldwell, NJ

Mar 18 1837

June 24 1908

23. Benjamin Harrison

Mar 4 1889

Mar 3 1893

North Bend, OH

Aug 20 1833

Mar 13 1901

24. Grover Cleveland

Mar 4 1893

Mar 3 1897

Caldwell, NJ

Mar 18 1837

June 24 1908

	25. William McKinley	**26. Theodore Roosevelt**	**27. William H. Taft**	**28. Woodrow Wilson**
Took office	Mar 4 1897	Sept 14 1901	Mar 4 1909	Mar 4 1913
Left office	**Sept 14 1901•**	Mar 3 1909	Mar 3 1913	Mar 3 1921
Birthplace	Niles, OH	New York, NY	Cincinnati, OH	Staunton, VA
Birth date	Jan 29 1843	Oct 27 1858	Sept 15 1857	Dec 28 1856
Death date	Sept 14 1901	Jan 6 1919	Mar 8 1930	Feb 3 1924

	33. Harry S. Truman	**34. Dwight D. Eisenhower**	**35. John F. Kennedy**	**36. Lyndon B. Johnson**
Took office	Apr 12 1945	Jan 20 1953	Jan 20 1961	Nov 22 1963
Left office	Jan 20 1953	Jan 20 1961	**Nov 22 1963•**	Jan 20 1969
Birthplace	Lamar, MO	Denison, TX	Brookline, MA	Johnson City, TX
Birth date	May 8 1884	Oct 14 1890	May 29 1917	Aug 27 1908
Death date	Dec 26 1972	Mar 28 1969	Nov 22 1963	Jan 22 1973

	41. George Bush	**42. Bill Clinton**	**43. George W. Bush**	
Took office	Jan 20 1989	Jan 20 1993	Jan 20 2001	
Left office	Jan 20 1993	Jan 20 2001	—	
Birthplace	Milton, MA	Hope, AR	New Haven, CT	
Birth date	June 12 1924	Aug 19 1946	July 6 1946	
Death date	—	—	—	

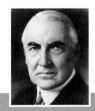

29. Warren G. Harding	30. Calvin Coolidge	31. Herbert Hoover	32. Franklin D. Roosevelt
Mar 4 1921	Aug 2 1923	Mar 4 1929	Mar 4 1933
Aug 2 1923•	Mar 3 1929	Mar 3 1933	**Apr 12 1945•**
Blooming Grove, OH	Plymouth, VT	West Branch, IA	Hyde Park, NY
Nov 21 1865	July 4 1872	Aug 10 1874	Jan 30 1882
Aug 2 1923	Jan 5 1933	Oct 20 1964	Apr 12 1945

37. Richard M. Nixon	38. Gerald R. Ford	39. Jimmy Carter	40. Ronald Reagan
Jan 20 1969	Aug 9 1974	Jan 20 1977	Jan 20 1981
Aug 9 1974★	Jan 20 1977	Jan 20 1981	Jan 20 1989
Yorba Linda, CA	Omaha, NE	Plains, GA	Tampico, IL
Jan 9 1913	July 14 1913	Oct 1 1924	Feb 11 1911
Apr 22 1994	—	—	—

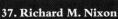

• Indicates the president died while in office.

★ Richard Nixon resigned before his term expired.

Index

About the Author

Don Nardo is a historian and award-winning writer who has published numerous books about American history. Among these are *The Declaration of Independence*, *The War of 1812*, *The Mexican-American War*, *The Indian Wars: From Frontier to Reservation*, *The Bill of Rights*, *The Great Depression*, and biographies of Thomas Jefferson and Franklin D. Roosevelt. He has included in this biography of Johnson many primary (original) quotations by the embattled president and his contemporaries. These give the reader a glimpse into the thoughts and personal feelings of one of the most controversial and fascinating figures in American history.